Fact or Opinion?

Workbook

Happy Frog Press

First Printing, 2017
ISBN 978-1-7752852-0-5
Happy Frog Press
www.HappyFrogPress.com

Introduction

Welcome to the "Fact or Opinion?" workbook! Inside you'll find 68 pages of worksheets to help children learn the difference between facts and opinions.

All kids need to know how to identify whether what they read is a fact or someone's opinion. This skill is especially important as they reach the age of accessing information from the internet.

In this workbook, this vital skill is built incrementally. Early pages focus on thinking about how to prove a fact/opinion and also how to identify the clue words that are indicative of a fact or an opinion. Later levels introduce the concept of false facts.

Our workbooks are designed to appeal to unmotivated learners. We use a colorful design, large print and lots of white space. We wish you and your learner all the best!

Additional Resources

Students often benefit from using a variety of resources that target the same skill. The variety allows them to maintain a higher interest level and consolidate their learning.

Happy Frog has a complementary "Fact or Opinion?" app that can help your learner. The app is available for Apple and Android devices.

We recommend using both apps and workbooks as the apps:

- Give instant feedback.
- Include an engaging Reward Center to motivate students.
- Allow independent use.
- Most of all... kids LOVE screen time. So life will be easier for you!

You can find out more about our reading comprehension and social skills apps and workbooks at www.HappyFrogApps.com

About Happy Frog Press

Happy Frog Apps & Happy Frog Press create high-quality resources for elementary-aged children with autism and other social/language challenges.

We believe that all children can learn – as long as we provide a learning environment that suits their needs.

www.Facebook.com/HappyFrogApps

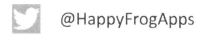
@HappyFrogApps

www.HappyFrogApps.com

,

A FACT is a statement that can be proven to be true or false.

Choose the fact:

Jack has a dog named Bingo.

Bingo is a nice dog.

Choose the fact:

My favorite star is the North Star.

There are stars in the sky.

A FACT is a statement that can be proven to be true or false.

Choose the fact:

Hummingbirds can fly backwards.

Hummingbirds are so cute.

Choose the fact:

I like animals that eat grass.

Some animals eat grass.

A FACT is a statement that can be proven to be true or false.

Choose the fact:

Cars can drive fast or slow.

Cars are too expensive.

Choose the fact:

People eat many types of plants.

Fruit is boring.

A FACT is a statement that can be proven to be true or false.

Choose the fact:

My team is the best.

My team has eleven players.

Choose the fact:

Carol invited me to her party.

There will be too many people at the party.

An OPINION is a person's belief about something.

Choose the opinion:

Reading is enjoyable.

Some books have pictures.

Choose the opinion:

A baseball game has two teams.

Baseball is a boring game.

An OPINION is a person's belief about something.

Choose the opinion:

Cheetahs are amazing animals to watch.

Cheetahs live in Africa.

Choose the opinion:

A hot dog has a sausage and a bun.

Hot dogs taste better than pizza.

An OPINION is a person's belief about something.

Choose the opinion:

If you visit Paris, you must see the Eiffel Tower.

The Eiffel Tower is located in France.

Choose the opinion:

There are two bags of candy on the table.

Candy is too sweet.

An OPINION is a person's belief about something.

Choose the opinion:

The math homework is due tomorrow.

I'll never get the math homework done.

Choose the opinion:

Dogs always look happy.

Turtles lay more than one egg.

Jim's cat has a black tail.

How can you prove this fact?

I can prove this by thinking about it.

I can prove this by showing you the cat.

Koalas only eat leaves.

How can you prove this fact?

_____

Camels have one or two humps.

How can you prove this fact?

I can prove it by looking in a book.

I know it's true because someone told me.

This can of soda has sugar in it.

How can you prove this fact?

_____

Most of the pizzas on this table have cheese.

How can you prove this fact?

By counting the pizzas with cheese and those without.

Because I love pizza.

The sun rose at 6:49 a.m. this morning.

How can you prove this fact?

_____

$$2 + 4 = 6$$

How can you prove this fact?

I can prove this because it makes sense.

I can prove this by counting.

Some children's books have pictures of fairies.

How can you prove this fact?

_____

Cauliflower is better than broccoli.

I think this is an opinion because...

People differ on what they think is better.

I am always right.

Cats are never happy.

I think this is an opinion because...

_____

Everyone should be interested in anatomy.

I think this is an opinion because...

'Should' is an opinion word.

Someone told me.

Comets are the most beautiful things in space.

I think this is an opinion because...

_____

My favorite burger is the Big Mac.

I think this is an opinion because...

Favorite things are opinions.

I read it on the internet.

Crows are more interesting than eagles.

I think this is an opinion because...

_____

All skateboarders are lazy.

I think this is an opinion because...

I saw it in a book.

'Lazy' is an opinion word. You and I might have different definitions of what is lazy.

Worms do not make good pets.

I think this is an opinion because...

_____

Winter is the most fun season.

I think this is an opinion because...

What I find fun might be different from what you find fun.

My mom told me.

My mom planted roses in the back yard.

I can prove this fact by:

_____

That coat has a blue collar.

I can prove this fact by...

Telling you it's true.

Showing you the coat.

Friday is the best day of the week.

I think this is an opinion because...

_____

People should have gardens.

I think this is an opinion because...

I learned it at school.

'Should' is an opinion word.

Oranges are round.

I can prove this fact by:

_____

Worms are sometimes brown.

I can prove this fact by:

Thinking about it.

Showing you some worms that are brown.

Cats are unfriendly.

I think this is an opinion because...

_____

Facts have CLUE WORDS that can be proven.

Which words suggest a fact?

I think

Comes after

Which words suggest a fact?

Dig

My favorite

Facts have CLUE WORDS that can be proven.

Which words suggest a fact?

Comes from

I believe

Which words suggest a fact?

Eats meat

Strangest teacher

Facts have CLUE WORDS that can be proven.

Which words suggest a fact?

Are black and white

Aren't polite

Which words suggest a fact?

Too many

Is planned

Facts have CLUE WORDS that can be proven.

Which words suggest a fact?

Are the prettiest

Have a sensitive sense of smell

Which words suggest a fact?

Is blue

Is happy

Opinions have CLUE WORDS that indicate people might have different thoughts.

Which words suggest an opinion?

Is boring

Is in December

Which words suggest an opinion?

Best

Are a type of bird

Opinions have CLUE WORDS that indicate people might have different thoughts.

Which words suggest an opinion?

Can bite

Most fun

Which words suggest an opinion?

Is too cold

Is frozen

Opinions have CLUE WORDS that indicate people might have different thoughts.

Which words suggest an opinion?

Has thorns

Wonderful

Which words suggest an opinion?

I think

Can keep you dry

Opinions have CLUE WORDS that indicate people might have different thoughts.

Which words suggest an opinion?

Can climb

Makes me happy

Which words suggest an opinion?

I will never

Is a type of soda

Let's practice more CLUE WORDS.

Which words suggest an opinion?

Annoying

Is made of

Which words suggest a fact?

Fantastic

Is standing

Let's practice more CLUE WORDS.

Which words suggest an opinion?

Are made of plastic

Are too hard

Which words suggest a fact?

Ugliest building

Oldest building

Let's practice more CLUE WORDS.

Which words suggest an opinion?

Is one of the 50 states

Is the least interesting state

Which words suggest a fact?

Lost her coat

Too loud

Let's practice more CLUE WORDS.

Which words suggest an opinion?

Is easy

Are filled with

Which words suggest a fact?

I would like

Is a group

Facts can be proven true OR false.

Select the true fact.

Candy bars are a type of fruit.

Candy bars are a sweet treat.

Select the true fact.

A hurricane is a very strong storm.

Hurricanes have slow winds.

Facts can be proven true OR false.

Select the true fact.

People usually have two arms.

I have ten arms.

Select the true fact.

Baseball is played on a football field.

Baseball is played on a baseball diamond.

Facts can be proven true OR false.

Select the true fact.

This glass table can fly.

The glass table is square.

Select the true fact.

Skateboards have four wheels.

Skateboards have twenty wheels.

Facts can be proven true OR false.

Select the true fact.

This test has 2000 questions and will take 10 minutes

This test has seven questions.

Select the true fact.

It rained here yesterday.

It rained books here yesterday.

Facts can be proven true OR false.

Select the false fact.

My TV is 50 inches wide.

My TV is wider than my living room.

Select the false fact.

My dentist has four legs.

My dentist has an assistant named Maria.

Facts can be proven true OR false.

Select the false fact.

Jupiter is under the ocean.

Jupiter is the largest planet.

Select the false fact.

Ears are used for listening.

Your nose is used for listening.

Facts can be proven true OR false.

Select the false fact.

Swimming is a water sport.

Swimming is done with skis.

Select the false fact.

A tree is an animal.

A tree is a living thing.

Facts can be proven true OR false.

Select the false fact.

Broccoli is a vegetable.

Broccoli is a type of meat.

Select the false fact.

Piano lessons teach you how to sing.

Piano lessons teach you to play the piano.

Butterflies are very pretty.

Fact or opinion?

Fact   Opinion

Two children are playing outside now.

Fact or opinion?

Fact   Opinion

Soccer is played using a ball.

Fact or opinion?

Fact   Opinion

Mr Taylor is the tallest teacher at school.

Fact or opinion?

Fact   Opinion

Playing video games is more fun than doing homework.

Fact or opinion?

Fact   Opinion

Monday is my favorite day of the week.

Fact or opinion?

Fact   Opinion

Red jelly beans taste the worst.

Fact or opinion?

Fact   Opinion

The new museum is on Smith Street.

Fact or opinion?

Fact   Opinion

Janice loves her new shoes.

Fact or opinion?

Fact   Opinion

A hot air balloon travels through the air.

Fact or opinion?

Fact   Opinion

Oranges should be eaten at breakfast and lunch.

Fact or opinion?

Fact   Opinion

Blue whales have nice skin.

Fact or opinion?

Fact   Opinion

That moon is called Pilates.

Fact or opinion?

Fact   Opinion

Friday comes after Thursday.

Fact or opinion?

Fact   Opinion

The church is the most beautiful building in town.

Fact or opinion?

Fact   Opinion

Butterflies are insects.

Fact or opinion?

Fact   Opinion

Today's temperature is the hottest so far this week.

Fact or opinion?

Fact   Opinion

Today is too hot.

Fact or opinion?

Fact   Opinion

This food smells awful!

Fact or opinion?

Fact   Opinion

Giant tortoises are bigger than cats.

Fact or opinion?

Fact   Opinion

The tail of a comet always points away from the sun.

Fact or opinion?

Fact   Opinion

Hummingbirds are the largest animal in the world.

Fact or opinion?

Fact   Opinion

The first day of school is scary.

Fact or opinion?

Fact   Opinion

The first day of school is September 4.

Fact or opinion?

Fact   Opinion

Select the fact.

Shopping is fun.

Winter skiing is done on snow.

Is that fact a true fact or a false fact?

True fact   False fact

Select the opinion.

Everyone has a birthday in January.

Dinosaurs are cool!

Select the fact.

Umbrellas can keep you dry.

I think umbrellas are useless.

Is that fact a true fact or a false fact?

True fact   False fact

Select the opinion.

Skateboarders are not polite.

Butterflies have scales on their wings.

Select the fact.

I will never be able to sew well.

Sewing uses a needle and thread.

Is that fact a true fact or a false fact?

True fact   False fact

Select the opinion.

A bike has five wheels.

Pandas should be left alone.

Select the fact.

I don't want it to rain.

It rained for three hours yesterday.

Is that fact a true fact or a false fact?

True fact   False fact

Select the opinion.

I broke my arm two years ago.

Watching fireworks is a lot of fun.

Select the fact.

Being a hockey goalie is easy.

Wolves dig with their paws.

Is that fact a true fact or a false fact?

True fact   False fact

Select the opinion.

Some cups are made of glass.

Crocodiles have too many teeth.

Select the fact.

Blue and yellow make green.

We think Selina stole the candy bar.

Is that fact a true fact or a false fact?

True fact   False fact

Select the opinion.

Cake is my favorite food.

We need food in order to live.

Select the fact.

Dogs are the best pet.

Dogs pant when they are hot.

Is that fact a true fact or a false fact?

True fact   False fact

Select the opinion.

Mrs Morton is a good teacher.

On average Giant Tortoises live longer than humans.

Select the fact.

My mom hates Fridays.

Friday comes after Saturday.

Is that fact a true fact or a false fact?

True fact   False fact

Select the opinion.

This chair is more comfortable than that one

This chair is more than 100 years old.

Select the facts.

☐ A goanna is a reptile from Australia.

☐ November is too cold and wet for me.

☐ November usually has more than 10 rainy days.

☐ People should be kinder to each other.

Select the opinions.

☐ A hockey goalie stops the puck from going into the net.

☐ I want to be a hockey goalie.

☐ Hockey is the best sport.

☐ Two teams play each other in hockey.

Select the facts.

☐ All dinosaurs are extinct.

☐ All students should watch the stars at night.

☐ All cats are black.

☐ All my cards are better than yours.

Select the opinions.

☐ Amanda loves her new shoes.

☐ My birthday party will be fun.

☐ Someone sewed the hole in my pants.

☐ That jacket is yours.

Select the facts.

☐ Your cat is crazy.

☐ This brown shirt is pink.

☐ Your teacher is sick today.

☐ Your coach is running late.

Select the opinions.

☐ Snakes shed their skin as they grow.

☐ I think it will rain today.

☐ The Weather Network says it will rain today.

☐ I don't want it to rain.

Select the facts.

☐ The car would look better if it were red.

☐ The party is scheduled from 3-5pm.

☐ Kyla is carrying skates, so she must be going skating.

☐ Umbrellas are used to do math.

Select the opinions.

☐ Fireworks are too loud.

☐ Fireworks are over too quickly.

☐ Fireworks explode in the sky.

☐ I can't wait to see the fireworks.

Answer Key

Page 4	Jack has a dog named Bingo	There are stars in the sky.
Page 5	Hummingbirds can fly backward.	Some animals eat grass.
Page 6	Cars can drive fast or slow.	People eat many types of plants.
Page 7	My team has eleven players.	Carol invited me to her party.
Page 8	Reading is enjoyable	Baseball is a boring game.
Page 9	Cheetahs are amazing animals to watch.	Hot dogs taste better than pizza
Page10	If you visit Paris, you should see the Eiffel Tower.	Candy is too sweet.
Page 11	I'll never get the math homework done.	Dogs always look happy.
Page 12	I can prove this by showing you the cat.	I can show you a book about koalas.
Page 13	I can prove it by looking in a book.	I can look at the ingredient list.
Page 14	By counting the pizzas with cheese and those without cheese.	I can show you the sunrise and sunset times in the newspaper or on the internet.
Page 15	I can prove this by counting.	I can show you some children's books with pictures of fairies.
Page 16	People differ on what they think is better.	No one can really tell whether a cat is happy or not. We can only guess.
Page 17	'Should' is an opinion word.	What I think is beautiful might be different from what you think is beautiful.
Page 18	Favorite things are opinions.	What I think is interesting might be different from what you think is interesting.
Page 19	'Lazy' is an opinions word. You and I might have different opinions of what is lazy.	You and I might have different ideas about what is a good pet.

Page 20	What I find fun might be different from what you find fun.	I can show you the rose bush in the back yard.
Page 21	Showing you the coat.	What you think is the best day might be different from what I think is the best day.
Page 22	'Should' is an opinion word.	I can show you an orange.
Page 23	Showing you worms that are brown.	You and I might have different ideas about what is unfriendly.
Page 24	Comes after	Dig
Page 25	Comes from	Eats meat
Page 26	Are black and white	Is planned
Page 27	Has a sensitive sense of smell.	Is blue
Page 28	Is boring	Best
Page 29	Most fun	Is too cold
Page 30	Wonderful	I think
Page 31	Makes me happy	I will never
Page 32	Annoying	Is Standing
Page 33	Are too hard	Oldest building
Page 34	Is the least interesting state	Lost her coat
Page 35	Is easy	Is a group
Page 36	Candy bars are a sweet treat.	A hurricane is a very strong storm.
Page 37	I broke my arm two years ago.	Baseball is played on a baseball diamond.
Page 38	The glass table is square.	Skateboards have four wheels
Page 39	This test has seven questions.	It rained here yesterday.
Page 40	My TV is wider than my living room.	My dentist has four legs.
Page 41	Jupiter is under the ocean.	Your nose is used for listening.
Page 42	Swimming is done with skis.	A tree is an animal.
Page 43	Broccoli is a type of meat.	Piano lessons teach you to sing.
Page 44	Opinion	Fact

Page 45	*Fact*	*Fact*
Page 46	*Opinion*	*Opinion*
Page 47	*Opinion*	*Fact*
Page 48	*Opinion*	*Fact*
Page 49	*Opinion*	*Opinion*
Page 50	*Fact (false fact)*	*Fact*
Page 51	*Opinion*	*Fact*
Page 52	*Fact*	*Opinion*
Page 53	*Opinion*	*Fact*
Page 54	*Fact*	*Fact (false fact)*
Page 55	*Opinion*	*Fact*
Page 56	*Winter skiing is done on snow. True.*	*Dinosaurs are cool!*
Page 57	*Umbrellas can keep you dry. True.*	*Skateboarders are not polite.*
Page 58	*Sewing uses a needle and thread. True.*	*Pandas should be left alone.*
Page 59	*It rained for 3 hours yesterday. True or false, depending on where you live.*	*Watching fireworks is a lot of fun.*
Page 60	*Wolves dig with their paws. True.*	*Crocodiles have too many teeth.*
Page 61	*Blue and yellow make green. True.*	*Cake is my favorite food.*
Page 62	*Dogs pant when they are hot. True.*	*Mrs Morton is a good teacher.*
Page 63	*Friday comes after Saturday. False.*	*This chair is more comfortable than that one.*
Page 64	*A goanna is a reptile from Australia.*	*November usually has more than 10 rainy days.*
Page 64	*I want to be a hockey goalie.*	*Hockey is the best sport.*
Page 65	*All dinosaurs are extinct.*	*All cats are black. (false fact)*
Page 65	*Amanda loves her new shoes.*	*My birthday party will be fun.*
Page 66	*This brown shirt is pink. (false fact)*	*Your teacher is sick today.* *Your coach is running late*
Page 66	*I think it will rain today.*	*I don't want it to rain.*

Page 67	*The party is scheduled from 3-5pm.*	*Umbrellas are used to do math. (false fact)*
Page 67	*Fireworks are too loud.*	*Fireworks are over too quickly.* *I can't wait to see the fireworks.*

Made in the USA
San Bernardino, CA
07 March 2018